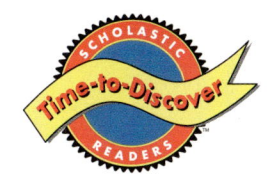

Owls Live in Trees

Melvin and Gilda Berger

SCHOLASTIC INC.
New York Toronto London Auckland Sydney
Mexico City New Delhi Hong Kong Buenos Aires

Photographs: Cover: Byron Jorjorian/Bruce Coleman, Inc., New York; p. 1: Joe McDonald/Bruce Coleman, Inc.; p. 3: Byron Jorjorian/Bruce Coleman, Inc.; p. 4: Ken Johns/Photo Researchers, New York; p. 5: Michael Giannechini/Photo Researchers; p. 6: John Hyde/Bruce Coleman, Inc.; p. 7: Jany Sauvanet/Photo Researchers; p. 8: Anthony Mercieca/Dembinsky Photo Associates, Owosso, MI; p. 9: Kenneth W. Fink/Photo Researchers; p. 10: Stephen J. Krasemann/Photo Researchers; p. 11: C. K. Lorenz/Photo Researchers; p. 12: Barbara Gerlach/Dembinsky Photo Associates; p. 13: Bill Lea/Dembinsky Photo Associates; p. 14: E. R. Degginger/Photo Researchers; p. 15: Jen & Des Bartlett/Bruce Coleman, Inc; p. 16: Ernest A. Janes/Bruce Coleman, Inc.

Book design by Annette Cyr

No part of this publication may be reproduced in whole or in part, or stored in a retrieval system, or transmitted in any form or by any means, electronic, mechanical, photocopying, recording, or otherwise, without written permission of the publisher. For information regarding permission, write to Scholastic Inc., Attention: Permissions Department, 557 Broadway, New York, NY 10012.

ISBN 0-439-47178-8

Text copyright © 2003 by Melvin and Gilda Berger
All rights reserved. Published by Scholastic Inc.
SCHOLASTIC, SCHOLASTIC TIME-TO-DISCOVER READERS, and associated logos are trademarks and/or registered trademarks of Scholastic Inc.

12 11 10 9 8 7 6 5 4 3 2 1   3 4 5 6 7 8/0

Printed in the U.S.A.
First printing, January 2003

Owls live in trees.

Fun Fact

Most owls live in hollow tree holes or old bird nests. They hunt for food at night.

Owls make nests in trees.

Owls live in nests made by other birds.

Fun Fact
Farmers like owls because they eat mice, rats, and other pests.

Owls live in barns.

Owls make nests in barns.

Fun Fact

Most owls that live on the ground hunt by day and by night.

Owls live on the ground.

Owls make nests on the ground.

Fun Fact
Burrowing owls often live in holes in the ground dug by other animals.

Owls live under the ground.

Owls make nests under the ground.

Fun Fact
The great gray owl is the biggest owl of all. It is more than 2 feet tall!

Owls live in tree stumps.

Owls make soft nests.

Fun Fact
Some owls that live in cold places fly to warm areas in winter.

Owls live where it is cold.

Owls live where it is warm.

Owls live nearly everywhere!